Waves on Waves

By Michael Jack Simkin

WAVES ON WAVES

First edition. October 9, 2024.

ISBN: 979-8227419668

Written by Michael Jack Simkin.

Table of Contents

"If you bring forth what is within you,
what you bring forth will save you.
If you do not bring forth what is within you,
what you do not bring forth will destroy you."

Thomas

To Sally, my greatest teacher

Section 1 - Alpha

8–12 Hz

At the base of awareness
Sits a gateway to the subconscious
A state of relaxation
Imagination, visualisation and creativity
The eyes may be closed or open
We may be sitting or lying down
Dancing, being massaged
Or making love
Here there is awareness of bodily sensations
Thoughts flow quietly
Or maybe there is a daydream
In any case
We find ourselves
Safe, calm and awake
It feels blissful and otherworldly

To Truly Laugh

Over the years
He developed such
Clever deflections
And elaborate coping mechanisms
To avoid me
That I lived mostly in his shadow
Influencing him out of sight
Far more than I would
If he had just acknowledged me
And allowed himself to feel me again

In obscurity I was able
To grow large
And became drunk and powerful
On the tears that flowed
From his troubled soul

He didn't realise
That to become whole
I am necessary
And while I am
The reason for his fear
I am also his redemption
A sacred signal

He didn't appreciate

WAVES ON WAVES

That I would never let him go
I am here to stay
My purpose is to help him evolve
And return to his original state
In this I'm utterly committed
But oh boy
He's a tough nut to crack

I've had to keep on calling him
Relentlessly
And all the while he would not listen
He continued to make things worse
That's the way it goes

Today
Little by little
He's catching on that
I'm not quite as bad as he thinks
And his fear of my sting
Is far worse than the sting itself

Wanted: A Creative Storyteller

We are proud to announce that
We're looking for a creative storyteller
Who is passionate about crafting
Premium content for social media
And knows how to make
SaaS sexy

As our ideal candidate
You're a self-starter
A team player
A real wordsmith
Who's totally dedicated to your work

You have a deep love for big data
Breathe capital markets
And devour the latest developments
In cyber security

You don't mind travelling
At short notice
Nor working
Long and unusual hours
At high intensity
And you're glad
To always attend
Optional company events

WAVES ON WAVES

This is a rapid growth opportunity
In a fast changing environment
This job is onsite
And requires one year's
Previous experience

We care dearly
About out staff
And our country
And while our competitive salary
May not be enough
To pay your basic living costs
We really want you to join our team

You can be sure that
We're going to have lots of fun
Moving the goalposts
And moving them again
Each time redefining your role
And gradually reducing your self-worth
As we micromanage your arse
To your plastic chair

Please attach an example
Of your work to your application

I did and this is it

A Reductionist Approach

Lemons float
And limes sink
And Jeffrey Dahmer
Refused to eat victims
Who had tattoos
Because the ink
Made the flesh taste strange

Michael is on the ladder
On the roof
With the chainsaw
Cutting branches

The Moon is moving away from Earth
At a rate of four centimetres per year

Sunsets on Mars are blue
And the water we drink from the tap
May be many millions of years older
Than the solar system itself

With consciousness
Came fragmentation
Eater and the eaten
And ever since
Life has been

WAVES ON WAVES

Trying to piece itself
Back together

The Bearded Buddhist

If a Buddhist
Is looking for his mother
And a man with a beard
Is looking for his father
A bearded buddhist
Must be looking
For both his parents

In Search of the Universal

Sounds like a noble venture?
This may be less about
Dissolving duality
Or aligning with pure consciousness
And more about encapsulating issues
That everyone cares about
You know, shit people will share
On social media
Because while I talk about oneness
My search is also for validation
Fuelled by a tale I tell myself about
Having the soul of an artist
As though I'm weeping
Tears of blood on the keyboard
As I apply for another copywriting job
At a fintech startup on LinkedIn

The Dilettante

A jejune epigone
May sound erudite and sophisticated
Like mimetic suppositions
Or polysyllabic pontification
And this dilettante will insist you listen
To his prosaic poetry
Though he rarely reads anyone else's
He's too busy counting his likes

He'll also tell you he's a musician
But he doesn't bother
With minor details
Like the circle of fifths

And he'll reveal he's a warrior
Though he doesn't actually practise
Martial arts

He says he cares about Palestinian rights
But isn't involved in any form of activism
He claims to care about the environment
Though can't quite bring himself
To remember to take reusable shopping bags
To the supermarket

He goes from one ayahuasca gathering

WAVES ON WAVES

To the next
Talking about facing his pain
But never doing it

He's a bit like a camera on AliExpress
At first glance
He may look like the real deal
Though on closer inspection
He's a shell
Who shies away from concerted effort
Sweeps only the visible parts of the floor
And craves results without being committed
To walk the walk
Oh dear

An axe

I had an axe
To grind
I ground it
And ground it
Now there is
Only a stick

Transceivers of Light

We transceivers of light
Created in the image of the Creator
Are made with divinity
And in as much as
We are contained within this universe
It is contained within us
And yet
Divorced from Nature
We have become subdued
We have over-specialized
And rendered ourselves asinine
Maybe only a cataclysm can save us?

While there is still time
Let us admit our inauthenticity
Our collective cowardice
Our impassivity
And ultimate self-sabotage

Ye Lords of Chaos
Bring down this venal system
Save us from the masturbating
Malevolent miscreants
And crummy crud-monkeys
It will not be the first time
That you have wiped the slate clean

Zit Porn

I can feel a rare spot on my back
But cannot see it.
And I never forget the past champions

The enormous 1994 surprise
Behind my left ear
That popped
In the palm of my hand
In the sixth form common room
The moment I found it

There was the 1997 delight
In the bathroom
Late one friday night
That was almost invisible
Intuition led me to it
And as I squeezed
A thin trail of white string emerged
Followed by
A shocking explosion
That audibly hit the mirror

And in 2000 there was the ingrown hair
That I somehow missed
Until it was ripe
I found it while driving my Smart Car

WAVES ON WAVES

And had to stop
At Burtonwood Services on the M62
I went into the old fashioned bathroom
The taps were the same as in the synagogue
I squeezed it
And an enormous thick black hair emerged
Like one of those cassette players
That used to open slowly and smoothly
It was followed by a white volcano
And I squealed with excitement

On Youtube
There are videos of pimples popping
That have been viewed more than
100 million times

It is something primal
And preening is fundamental to apes
A caring act
That helps buy standing
In the group

The joy of popping zits
Also seems to lie in
Intermittent reinforcement
A feature common
In enjoyable activities
Where tension is followed by release
Like gambling, strenuous exercise, fasting
Sex and having a shit

All the Work

All the work
Intimacy
And love making
Hours sat on the cushion
Lying on the mat
Sessions with the therapist
Turning on the massage bed
Sitting in groups
Passing conch shells
Being extra vulnerable
Releasing blocked emotions
Acknowledging that the other
Is not the other
The fact remains
When stress levels rise
Awareness goes out of the window
Leaving me cursing
And wishing for the death
Of the guy
Who cut me up
On the roundabout

Yonatan said
See the connection
Between thought
Speech
And action

WAVES ON WAVES

- Clean the temple
Well, the temple
Has some tough-to-remove
Muck on the floor

Peel the Onion

For Günter Grass it is
Never too late to confront the past
To reach forgiveness
And the possibility of redemption
Through art

And Wendy Orr knows
Never to give up on your dreams
Even in the darkest of times

Delving into the self
Or the anus
Towards the core
Foundations of being
Can bring tears to the eyes

And we keep on
Peeling away
Layer upon layer
Ultimately to find that
In the middle
There is nothing

Waves on Waves

- I've had one
- What's that, love?
- A fucking bravewave, darling!
- Well, don't burn a circuit

It's hard not to
When you contemplate
All the ups and downs
Endless rhythmic cycles
Radiating out in every direction
Bidding us to surrender to the waves
And bravely ride our incarnations
And the roles we play between dimensions

There is but one choice
That brings happiness
That is to love what is
Letting go

It's all waves on waves
Gravitational waves
Cosmic waves
Electromagnetic waves
Quantum waves
Sound waves
Mexican waves

MICHAEL JACK SIMKIN

Neural oscillations
And all the waves of experience
In the great ocean of consciousness

Bound within the boundless
Confined within these bodies
It is said that we move between five states
Depending on our level of
Wakefulness and activity
Knowing where we are at
May help us influence our mood

Can you turn inwards and feel
The synchronised electrical pulses
Of your neurons talking to each other?
Can you breathe with the waves?
Difficult waves
Easy waves
Can you rest floating in the sea
Of awareness that holds us
So gently we often do not feel it?

One frequency leads to another
It is a continuous song of consciousness
The waves change according to
What we're doing and feeling
In a neverending feedback loop
When slower brain waves prevail
Deep and loud like a drum
There may be feelings of
Tiredness, lethargy, or dreamyness
Higher frequencies

WAVES ON WAVES

Fast, subtle and complicated
Resonating with overtones
May be accompanied by feelings
Of alertness, being lit up
Or even samadhi

Section 2 - Beta

12.5 - 30 Hz

It is a state of alertness
Experienced in close concentration
And cognition
In problem solving
And looking to the outside world
With logic and reason

It can also arise with excitement and anxiety
Or when integrating new experiences
It is the favoured state of our teachers
Employers and political leaders

Some mistake this state
For being human
And miss out on the rest of
The majestic orchestra

Distant Thunder

An ominous and steady throbbing
In the heart
And an itchiness in the body
Call persistently
As I listen
To Tara Brach
Encouraging awareness
Of the body's field of sensations
There is the distant thunder
Of fighter jets above
It feels strangely
Like the eve of a holiday
As we wait for the missiles
And meanwhile my overdraft
Continues to grow
And what of those
On the other side of the fence?
What of the terror they feel?

To Those

To those who carved so precisely
The great diorite boxes of the Serappeum
Placing them inside such narrow chambers
How to make sense of your achievement?

To the gardeners of the Amazon
Did you drink Ayahuasca
And turn your visions into earthworks
As Uncle Graham suspects?

To those who quarried
The great stones of Baalbek's trilithon
How in heaven's name
Did you lift them?

To the architects and engineers of Luxor
Who gave you
Such colossal knowledge?

Let's not forget
The builders of Gunung Padang,
Karahan Tepe, Ollantaytambo and Pumapunku
And all the other miraculous places
How on Earth
Did you do it?

WAVES ON WAVES

Seems we know little more about our history
Than the bees do

An Urge

I'm holding a pen
Sitting in front of
A folded piece of paper
And limitless potential
With an urge
To fill space
With something meaningful
After learning that
A powerful gamma ray burst
Hit our Earth on Sunday
It travelled 1.4 billion years
Across the universe
Before entering our solar system
Potentially it was created
As a star collapsed
And a black hole was formed
It reached us
While we were eating dinner
Little do we realise
How lightly we are here

Bonobos

The queen is the centre of the group
And never had a bra to burn
She spends time with her girlfriends
Eating, socialising and grooming one another
Sometimes they embrace and
Rub their genitals together

Females are also open
To sexual activity with males
During the infertile periods of their cycle
While males do not know
When the females are fertile

The birth rate is low
And there tend to be
More females than males in a group
Meaning there is less pressure on males
To compete for and to control females
This leads to greater female freedom and power
And a peaceful atmosphere
Where squabbles rarely escalate

When a young female joins the group
She will form friendships
With older females to protect her

MICHAEL JACK SIMKIN

The queen or one of her friends
Shares out the food
Without monopolising it

Males may start to get restless
Drag around branches to get attention
And start trying to get others moving
But only when the queen feels like doing so
Do the rest of the group follow

Black Sheep

Like a goat
Sent out into the wilderness
On Yom Kippur
Bearing the sins of the Hebrews
I became a designated problem
The symbol of suffering

In exiling me
They exiled their pain
Was this your role too?

And did you manifest that pain?
And could they not stand
To see it either?

Heavenly Bodies

Seconds of the day
Degrees of the circle
Interior angles of platonic solids
Pythagoras' number of God
F# major
The Great Year
Abra fucking cadabra

When we measure
The speed of light and
Dimensions of heavenly bodies
Noting the distances between them
Using the old measurements
Derived from our bodies
You know
Inches, feet, yards and miles
For some reason
We see factors of
Four Hundred and Thirty Two
Again and again

We are also heavenly bodies
Made in the image of the universe
Fragile before cosmic forces
And bound to embrace death
While courageous in love

Formicidae

Unlike the great pyramids of power
That we have built around ourselves
Their colony works without central control
They have no leader
None tells the others what to do
And yet somehow they manage to build cities
And organise themselves in group activities
Apparently flocks of birds
Neurons, molecules
And people running blockchains
Do something similar

A Dark Light unto the Nations

We who struggle with God
Allowed exploitation and entitlement to be
A necessary byproduct of our need to survive
But now we are rich
In our devotion to Shekel
And what we tried to avoid
We have become
And we remain stuck
In our sympathetic nervous systems
With no peripheral vision
And little space to consider the needs of others
Integrity is lost from our dictionary
While we salute our flag with religious fervour
And justify our brutality
In this land of polemics and plastic tableware
We pray to our creator
Caring little about nature
Or collective responsibility
"But they hate us!" we cry
Have you ever stopped to think why?

If I had to Die, my Son

If I had to die, my son,
What message would I hope
To leave you?

I'd begin by saying that our love
Will not be broken because of my passing,
And although I'm leaving this world physically,
On the non-physical plane
I will always be with you.

And so, when you need me,
Close your eyes and imagine me.
This will allow us to connect,
So you can feel me
And know my spirit is with you.

About your relationship with yourself,
I say trust yourself,
Trust your heart and gut,
Try to do what you know is right,
But don't beat yourself up if you don't manage.

Use your intelligence and talents wisely,
For every moment is precious,
So don't get trapped in bullshit,
And don't presume too much

MICHAEL JACK SIMKIN

About anything, or anyone.

Be sceptical, yet still open,
Feel your way through life
More than thinking your way through it.
Remain with your breath
And the sensations in your body.

Do what you love,
Be playful,
And make your life an adventure.
Allow yourself to feel your pain,
Do not hide from it.
Life by its nature involves pain,
And often the fear of it
Is worse than the thing itself.

Remember that while I use words
To tell you these things,
Words are unlikely
Ever to explain the nature of the universe.
The deeper truth lies,
In experience itself,
In the feeling of being alive.

There are many doors into visionary states,
Where our sense of self may
Expand to include the whole world:
Meditation and yoga, plant medicine,
Tantra, long walks and fasting.
Explore them all, according to your preferences.
Know life deeply

Beyond thinking and social conditioning,
And give your soul its best chance to evolve.

What you believe about yourself,
Affects the way the world treats you.
Learn to accept all aspects of yourself completely.
In your relationships, be present and total,
Be close to those who see who you as you are,
And treat you with respect.
Remember that beyond outward appearances,
We are all part of one life.

You, my son, are the greatest gift I have been given,
Through you, I have tasted pure love.
You've given me a reason
To dig deeper and heal myself.
Through you, I am more complete.
And luckily,
I'm not planning on dying any time soon,
So the things that I've said to you here,
I can hopefully learn to do myself.

The Wind

Walking Lucky in the fields
Following the rain
After a baking hot summer
There is the smell of
Herbs
Bacteria
And ozone.

Stopping in my tracks
Allowing myself to feel the wind
The outside reaches in

Greater life touches me
It is immersive
A wake-up call
I can't ignore

The wind speaks only truth
The Hebrew for wind is *ruach*
The same word is used for spirit

We do not know where we come from
Nor where we are heading to

In this part of the world
Winds carry names

WAVES ON WAVES

Like the *Chamsin*
Which blows sand from the desert
In autumn and spring
On both sides of the fence

Deuteronomy 21:18-21

"If a man has a stubborn and rebellious son
who will not obey the voice of his father
or the voice of his mother, and,
though they discipline him,
will not listen to them,
then his father and his mother
shall take hold of him
and bring him out to the elders of his city
at the gate of the place where he lives,
and they shall say to the elders of his city,
'This our son is stubborn and rebellious;
he will not obey our voice;
he is a glutton and a drunkard.'
Then all the men of the city
shall stone him to death with stones.
So you shall purge the evil from your midst,
and all Israel shall hear, and fear.

Oh Shit, it's the Poetry Voice!

When I wrote these words
On the computer
And read them outloud
To myself
Off the screen
They felt so good
Well, mum did say I have talent

But now as I stand
In front of the microphone
And your glistening eyes
I hear the wavering in my voice
As I begin to read
Something sounds hollow
Devoid of significance
You seem to notice it too

I've overestimated my noetic ability
I've tried to fight above my weight
It is a case of self-inflicted poetic injustice

But I can't stop now
I must read
And read I do
And so I plead
Almost singing

In desperation
Stressing syllables
With rhythmic enforcement
So you cannot fail to notice
The music that plays out
Amid the meaning of my words

I need you to understand
Just how much I feel
Do not throw me away
But preserve me

Oh shit, it's the poetry voice
Only one step better than Liz Truss

My Mother is Dying

In video calls on Whatsapp
With my sister
Sitting next to my sleeping mother
I see life slowly leaving her
I feel it in my belly
A mute dread
Unresolved
Involuted emotions

She woke and told my sister
I let you down
My sister answered
That this was not the case
But she did let us down
She permitted my father's abuse
And used her own
Bizarre policy of divide and rule
And then she would be angry
When we didn't get on
And she pushed
Her brand of religion onto us
And her matrix of control and fear

But my mother was also my saviour
And when we were little
She encouraged creativity

And artistic expression
Inspiring my desire to write

She is Dead

Eden had arrived to look after Lucky
I was about to head to the airport
When my sister called
It's happening she said in tears
And pointed the camera at our mother
I heard her slow gasps
And saw her face so distorted
From the one I had known

Enjoy the ride mum
I said
I love you
And she breathed her last
With a slight gasp
And I felt her presence
Fill my being
In a way I had not felt
Since childhood
The feeling remained with me for hours
And Eden hugged me
Though we had only just met

It rained the next day at her funeral
Between tears I said that
She passed with my blessing
Anna made a speech

The rabbi slipped
And had to be taken away in an ambulance

At the *shiva*
My brother-in-law asked
Are we allowed to sit here?
It is your house, I said

And I listened to eulogies
And quickly found them
Hard to stomach

The next day my son said
Aba, she is dead, come home
And I did

Really, Very Good Friends

Hey friends
Consciousness
Wherever you are
On other planets
Moons and craft
Circling stars
Around distant galaxies
Inhabiting different dimensions
Just because we can't prove you exist
Doesn't mean you don't

I wonder
When you turn inside
Does the sensation of being alive
Feel to you as it does to me?

Do we share some of the same concerns?
Perhaps by allowing this connection
We can resonate
And if this is the case
Can you maybe help us
Save us from ourselves?
Maybe you've already tried?

Were some of you
The Benei Elohim

Or Viracocha?
And that time on DMT
Was it one of you who said
"Yippie, finally he's done it" ?
Was it you who told me I was welcome
And asked me if you could use me
To perform calculations?
And did you pass information through me?
Was I your data node?
Your relay?
And are you waiting for me
To return?

XKeyscore

Scrolling with our fingers
Our faces lit by screens
Tech has connected us
And provided us
A powerful means
To avoid ourselves

We nodes in the net
Overstimulated and weakened
Hey I even take
My phone to the toilet
So maybe the Amish
Aren't so nuts after all

As we advance
Healthy chaos is lost
And as we become
More specialised
We become more marginal and robotic
Long ago Zamyatin and Orwell already knew
Where we are heading

In China they are testing
Electronic headbands
On school kids
To check when they

Are concentrating on their work

How far will it go
Before this house of cards
Comes tumbling down?

What's your Mango?

After Chairman Mao
Gave mangoes
To workers
During the Cultural Revolution
A mango cult developed
Workers preserved mangoes
In formaldehyde
And made wax replicas
They worshipped mangoes
Holding processions to celebrate them
What's your mango?

Collective Stress

There have in the past
Been outbreaks of hysterical dancing,
Hysterical laughter and epidemics of suicide.
Of these the hysterical dancing appeals the most
If it broke out again
It would please me no end
Of course reality is probably far from the idea
And I wouldn't want anyone to get hurt
By dancing until their demise.
I wonder
What is this all about?
I guess it is a communal purging
Of collective stress.
Well, I'm waiting.

Are you Sirius?

After so long shrouding the earth
From the sun and the stars
The clouds eventually parted
And once again
The brightest star in the night sky was
Sirius

We tracked you
In the great new clarity
And built temples pointing towards you

And once again
The heavens were like a great eye
As we looked out
To see the mood of the universe
And ourselves

Did the wise men
Who survived the flood
Sail around the world
Teaching agriculture
Astronomy and architecture
To other survivors?
Did they build monuments
To commemorate what happened
To warn us that it could happen again?

The 1% of the 1%

Maybe the 1% of the 1%
Haven't yet read Ramana's Mind
They forgot our possessions own us
And knowledge is ignorance
Maybe it doesn't matter
They have rigged the game
And want to keep it this way
It's natural they do what they can
To exercise influence
And breathe together with friends

The infernal machine
Must roll on
And on it does
And the market
A beast of our creation
Is hungry to be fed
And bigger fish get bigger
By eating little fish
And the microplastic they contain

While they are busy
Developing their positions
Will the 1% of the 1%
Be too drunk on power
To recognise the great tsunami

WAVES ON WAVES

When it returns?
Their super bunkers in New Zealand
May be of little help
And the survivors
Who will take our species
Forward again
Will be the tribesmen
Who know
How to live close to the land

Do you know your Alphabet?

In every area of our lives
A corporation sits in the background

Have you seen those hierarchical
Quilts of logos
With symbols such as
General Mills, Danone,
And Associated British Food?
And who the fuck are Mondelez?
They used to be known as Kraft

The biggest institutional investors are
Said to be Vanguard
Blackrock, State Street Corporation and
Berkshire Hathaway
In some cases these companies
Also own each other's stock
So ultimately
Companies that appear to be competitors
Are not entirely so
The top of the the pile
Is Vanguard
A private company
So you can't see who the shareholders are
It's thought to be owned
By non-profit foundations

WAVES ON WAVES

Of the most influential families in the world
Such as the Bushes, Windsors, Rothschilds,
Morgans, Rockefellers, and Vanderbilts
Orsinis, Gates', Soros' and Clintons
The owners sit in the background
Managing unseen links between
Business, politics and media

These nonprofits have no need
To disclose who their donors are
And as long as their profits are reinvested
There are no taxes to pay
And thus the richest
Hide in plain sight

And while the screws slowly tighten
Maybe this is the quiet before the storm
As we glide on blindly towards the abyss
Staring at our screens
Forgetting that
The cost of not caring
For one another
And our world
Is far greater than
The cost of doing so

Geomagnetic Storms

Our sun is middle-aged and still gets spots sometimes, as he dances through space. Occasionally, the lines of his magnetic field get so tangled around these spots, they need to reorganise, and this causes sudden explosions of energy. It's a bit like he's popping a zit and farting in the process. And as he does so, radiation gets emitted, right across the spectrum, and great streams of high-energy particles, mostly protons, travel outwards from him through space, in all directions and at various speeds.

The timeframe of these occurrences is recorded in the rings of ancient trees and in our icecaps. From them it is clear that sporadically, often with thousands of years between major events, sudden beams of radiation ejected from the sun hit Earth, overwhelming our magnetic field and leaving lifeforms vulnerable and unprotected.

At times our ancestors were made sick by this radiation. Some managed to withdraw into caves or hide under dolmen. Was Derinkuyu made to protect against such episodes?

After an explosion on our sun, the first particles and protons of the solar wind to touch our magnetosphere would circle around our magnetic poles forming visible outer-rings. To man it looked like a cosmic crown in the heavens.

And as protons became trapped by Earth's magnetic field, they travelled down our polar cusps, colliding with and ionising atoms of oxygen and nitrogen in our atmosphere. The resulting plasma formed surreal structures of light in the skies - dazzling, beautiful and terrible aurora, visible from all parts of Earth,
even during the day.

And between the outer ring of plasma above each magnetic pole, two long trumpets of light reached down towards Earth's North and South Poles, twisting into two intense and opposing auroral funnels.

As the gas became compressed, a chain of spheres and a taurus appeared in the tubes of the trumpet shapes, and as the energy flowed stronger, the shapes merged. And where the plasma was densest, the charge would sometimes exceed capacity and become unstable. A shockwave would form and there would be sudden explosions in the heavens, flashes of electrical discharge, and beads of lightning would twist about, painting wisps of plasma in repeating fractal patterns. These may have lasted from days to decades. The highest energy plasma generated such powerful and stunning ultraviolet and X-ray radiation, it was enough to blind and even kill man.

We had to make sense of our suffering, and as we looked at these terrifying, gigantic animated structures of light in the sky, we saw them as the appearance of the Gods. Their messages were accompanied by great thunder that foretold death and destruction - punishment for our sins.

To process what was happening, man painted, carved, and pecked into rocks the stories he saw emerging above. And in this way, he immortalised them. Over generations, these original messages were preserved, added to and reinterpreted.

In the skies we saw a heavenly squatter, a stick man with two circles next to his sides. Sometimes he had the head of a duck. We saw bows and arrows, noses, eye brows, and facemasks. We saw caterpillars, ladders, and thunderbirds with their zapping beaks. We saw Inana, Goddess and femme fatal, clothed in radiance, beautiful and heartless, roaring like a dragon, and raining down fire on Earth. No creature could stand up to her. And we saw Horus as a small child, standing on two crocodiles, grasping scorpions, serpents, a lion and an antelope.

When the next solar storm occurs, we will learn about it eight minutes and twenty seconds later. Soon after, our electronics will be destroyed, and there will be little way to share warnings to take adequate cover. It's best to locate a suitable cave now, and purchase some extra dark goggles. And maybe it's time for me to start selling solar storm survival kits - so you too can make it the next time we get a visit from the Gods of Light.

Section 3 - Gamma
30-80 Hz

It is a magical state of insight
Peak focus and expanded consciousness
It occurs when the mind is quiet
When the dancer becomes the dance
El duende
It arises in love and devotion
Looking deeply into each others eyes
In union with nature
In shamanic states
In the zone

I am sorry

You have had to witness my struggle
Knowing I am only in this country
For you
And you have had to hear me complaining
Repeatedly
About the lack of common decency
Of these rapacious people
And I have said that elsewhere
I could have given you so much more
Community
A house on a lake
A boat
A deep connection to nature
And you knew it to be true
And it makes you feel bad
It makes you feel guilty
That I am stuck
And I am sorry for this
Know that it is my choice
To be here
And not yours
Love and accept yourself
Despite me
And do not follow me
In allowing yourself to feel trapped

Union

In union
Deeper purpose is realised
With soft power
Like rain falling on parched earth
And with courage to be here
Head and body align
Cosmic gates open
In sidereal majesty
It is a divine expression
Of poles united
As goddess and priest
Perform a rite
On behalf of creation
And it is registered
In the akashic records
Stick that in your pipe and smoke it

Perpetual Choice

What a spectrum to contain
Such contrast
Between moments of
Grace
Presence
And connection
Balanced on the blade of space-time
And at the other extreme
Gravity
Grim separation and
I'll get you mother fuckers
And between the two
The myriad degrees of duality

Drunk with Anger

Through Maya I saw that
I am drunk with anger
It is my addiction
And in bitterness I hide
From Eros
Mine is the voice of my father
Whose approval I so need
And though he passed long ago
I continue to live in his shadow

What matters is
Not the situation in Israel
It is loving my son

As an old man
I will beg to return
To these days
If only for a moment
Arguing with petty bureaucrats

While we can

We have been ravaged
Rendered
Petrified
Obliterated
Yet we have forgotten
And become complacent

Repeatedly
Times of calm and tranquillity
Have been smashed by
Solar storms
Polar switches
And planetary bodies colliding

Our species
Has been cast down
In a game of cosmic
Snakes and ladders

May this knowledge provide impetus
To live life fully
As it is
While we can

A Poem Written with Eyes Closed

Plastic keys clicking
Smooth under the fingertips
A car drives past
A distant voice speaks
An inner feeling of pride arises
For typing without looking at the screen
There's a slight tension in the belly and heart
A sense of something needing to be done
A dog barks
Sleeves rest on the arms
A memory of Robbe-Grillet returns
With a dull thud in the head
Breathing in
Feet touching
Energy circling
The back rests against the chair
Lips together
Left nostril a little blocked
The wind blows the leaves on the trees
A moment of stillness
A desire to be
With what is now
An unexpected burp

Primal

It's said that
In the womb
We already form beliefs
About we who are
What others will be for us
And what will be our place
In the world

And then we emerge
Grow conditioned
And forget
We are inseparable
From the source
We are life
Looking at itself

In old age
We last forget
What first we learn
Until as we breathe our last
A final picture forms in our minds

And knowledge
Knowledge leaves us
One step removed

WAVES ON WAVES

It is to the senses
We must listen
To the very feeling of aliveness
That whispers connection

And cleanly I will go
Without residue

Trajectory

Apparently our trajectory
Through soul-space isn't fixed
It can be changed

What blocks the way is
My anger that
I trusted
I would be protected
And was surprised
To find out
This wasn't the case

Before that
Is the blissful memory
Of looking out into the redness of the sun
Through my mother's belly
It looked like it does
When you look at the sun
Through closed eyes

Seems some born
By planned
Caesarean Section
Expect life
To be handed to them
On a plate

WAVES ON WAVES

I wonder if
Listening to the language of sensations
Is really enough?

And when we dare
To break our glass ceilings
It's best to wear
Safety glasses and a hard hat
To protect ourselves
From falling shards

Return

We are all fingers
On the hands of God
Rubbing against one another
Wiggle wiggle

Our eyes are Hers
Looking at Herself
And our thoughts
Are ruminations of
Her mind

Fear separates
And love unites

I end my exile
And return to the sea
Wiggle wiggle

Mob

Making decisions not my own,
Biochemical reactions,
Conditioned by formation,
Initiated with coercion ,
And assisted by propaganda.
Like the many,
I made the mistake of trading in freedom
For the security of the group.
I conformed to norms and traditions,
Stuck masks to my faces,
Covered up the pain of betrayal and abandonment
And the fear of surfing through the void
And loving without clinging on.

Section 4 - Delta

0.5 - 4Hz

In this state of detached awareness
The external world is gone
It is a time of healing and regeneration
A domain of compassion
Some who meditate
Can remain awake in this state
Most come here in deep
Dreamless sleep

The Inevitable Transition

How far is it to Derinkuyu?
Too far and the border is closed.
We shield our eyes from the blinding light
Drop to the ground
And cover our noses and mouths with cloths

I wonder if I will go gracefully
Or writhing in terror and misery?

Unhappy I cleave to life
Fulfilled I accept
The Inevitable transition

Breath

As a small child
I remember being bored at
King David Primary School
In Liverpool
Lying with my head on the desk
My eyes slightly above my hand
Closely examining the pores of my skin
As the sun shone down
Through the window
I imagined I was a pilot observing land
Far beneath the cockpit
For the most part
I had already forgotten
The voice in my heart
That quietly hums
The melody of the spheres
And the language of connection

Today I face the challenge
Of remaining with
Uncomfortable sensations
In my heart
And try to resist running away
To the same old lairs of thought
And I remind myself
That's okay too
Field and spirit

Are one and the same

Fleeting

I have a fleeting memory
As a baby
That reality could feel overwhelming
I didn't know where to put myself
And I cried
Sometimes those cries went unanswered
That's how things were done back then

Later I recall
Trying to understand the difference
Between Michael and Simkin
Liverpool, England and Jewish

I remember my mother's cuddles
And climbing into my parents' bed
Dad spelled like farts
Mum like flowers
Dad was insulted
I wouldn't cuddle him

I remember occasionally
He would pick me up
Put me on his shoulders
Run around the house
Jump onto the bed
Then dangle me

WAVES ON WAVES

Over the bannister
And I would squeal with real fear
As well as her hugs and kisses
I remember my mother's anger
And her slaps
Put on your smiling face
I would tell her
I remember
Her look of fear
The morning
Dad had a heart attack
She said it was okay
But I knew it wasn't

Some years later
Dad hit me with his belt
Mum promised her protection
But did not dare to give it

At school I kept the bullying
A secret
And did not ask for help

When my lower back fell apart
I feared losing my legs
Feared I would never know sex

And as a teen I longed for girls
Felt frozen
And did not know what to say
Of course
It is not the sob story that counts

Rather the internalised pain
That was repressed for survival
And needs release

And I look up from the computer
Out through the kitchen window
At the bougainvillaea
Growing over the fence
In the afternoon sun
So purple and so white
It almost looks artificial
And down the road
The trees cast shadows
Across the field
While in front of me
The branches of the olive tree
Sway in the breeze
In the living room
The ceiling fan is turning
It doesn't really need to be on
I turn it off and am quiet

Flames

In early spring
I burned the skin of a snake
And sprinkled
Some of the ash in my eyes
From burnt
Destruction and pain
Flickered an ember of eternal light
On Earth
Bound by gravity
Flames
Are like teardrops
Cone-shaped and symmetrical
In space
Hot air expands
But does not move upwards
So flames are spherical
Like little suns

Sativa

When I vaped sativa
My heart rate would increase
With this arose a sense of acceleration
And with it anxiety
It felt like I was being pushed down the road
Rather than walking down it
Was this Spirit pointing me towards
My blindspots?
Bidding me to return to the body
To allow myself to feel emotional pain?

And I remind myself that others are not other
And unity and bliss are located
On the other side of the door
On which is written is fear

I See that I See

Eyes closed
I see
Vibrating red
Pixels
Aliveness
Silent God
Touching thumb and second finger
Warm waves sweep the body
With a slight smile
It happens again
Fuckin' Zen
Baba

Moments Before Waking

As I stand at tall
Wooden doors
Intricately carved
Grand with the promise of
What lies on the other side
I want the guts
To add the letter n to the word waking
In the title of this poem

The handle is heavy
There is trepidation
But I know I have to turn it
And will walk through

I've been here before
In a space
Build from heavenly matter
That scintillates against darkness
Beyond things and nothings
And I sense home

Orbit

How stultifying and stifling
How murderous to presence
To be trapped
In a money making spiral
Whose curve is described
By shame, self doubt
And financial anxiety
Whose tight orbit
Is an infernal treadmill
Like the childhood experience
Of inescapable abuse

When there was no one
To share my pain with
I spoke through my actions
Why are you hurting me?
You are supposed to love me as I am
And as you do not
I will not love myself either
And as I cannot exist without you
The problem must be me
I am not okay
And to become so
I must deserve to be punished
Again and again

A Porcupine

I dreamed I was a porcupine
Who harboured memories of
Being human.
I faced a choice -
To accept the situation and make the most of it,
Or continue struggling to return to being a man.
There was no magic button to press with my paws,
And as I walked
I kept catching my quills on plants and bushes.
I could find few advantages to being a porcupine
Though I found
Tree bark was tasty to chew.
And then
Walking down the path you came
And stopped before me
You were not afraid to kiss me
And I awoke.

Kokorozashi

Autumn excitement
Rotting ruddy leaves
And the smell of leather
Gazing into each other's eyes
Revealing unconditioned beasts
An unsatisfiable hunger
Used to stand
In the way of presence
Now I say to myself
You got what you wanted
Live with it
And I face a new subject
- Living with what I thought I wanted

Note to Self

Nowhere to get to
No one to be
Nothing to attain
In presence
Focus changes
There is only Love
When I don't see this
I live on the fumes of hope
A wet fart on the meditation cushion

Section 5 - Theta

4 - 8Hz

It is an ephemeral state of bliss
That arises as we wake
And drift off to sleep
It is a vivid and visionary state of meditation,
Of deepest relaxation and hypnosis,
Dreamy, trippy and fleeting.
It is a space of intuition and remembering
Where we are connected to our shadows
And withdrawn from the external world.

My Greatest Teacher

Into your trap
I walked unprotected
Allowed you to trick me
When your period had ended
Later you threw the pregnancy test
In the bin saying it was negative
I picked it out to check
And saw it was positive

You insisted on bringing
Our child into the world
"You have nothing to worry about," you said.

My friends told me I did not have to stay
We were not a couple and
I am not Israeli
Nor do I feel part of this brutal land

But I could not leave
Knowing I had a child
Who I imagined would be brought up
With little awareness of higher functioning
Art or integrity
I could not face the idea of
Meeting him aged sixteen
And not being able to know who he was

WAVES ON WAVES

Still traumatised from childhood
I was unclear about my boundaries
And didn't yet know how to love myself
This is probably why
I needed to face
An inescapable double-bind
Where you would be able
To make my life insufferable
So as a matter of survival
I would be forced to turn within
And face every part of myself
Rather than be made sick
By my dreadful thoughts

I have learned the meaning of
Mixed emotions
For while our son is a wondrous being
And we share fun and meaningful times
Misery hangs heavily in my heart
As I feel trapped in Israel because of you
And I am wasting away
My dreams of building a farm
Of being surrounded by like-minded people
Becomes increasingly unrealistic
And I face the middle of middle age
Invisible and unappreciated
Stuck in financial anxiety

And I remember how free
I used to be in Asia
And in many beautiful parts of the world

MICHAEL JACK SIMKIN

Where the inheritance I received
Would have been enough
For a home and a project of the heart

And all the while
You see your own struggle
You do not appreciate that
I did not run away
You are too busy culturing your image
Of the single mother
Who does not have any help
Despite your sisters and parents
And our son being with me half the time

For the past twelve years
You have blamed me for your loneliness
And tried to make me pay
For rejecting you
Even when damaging me
Meant damaging our son
And you feel entitled to exploit me
To take my presence and my money
In any way you can
While you've also tried
To take our son for yourself
You refuse to share information
And cooperate

Just as your father could not see you
You chose me who would not see you either
And as my parents could not see me
I chose you who would not either

WAVES ON WAVES

And so this circular mirror
Created a new generation
Like a lotus flower born in mud

Before our son came to this world
My attempts at healing were
At best half hearted
My sense of self was so damaged
That I did not think I was worth fixing
It is only through the
Pure love for my child
That I have dug deeper
So generational wounds
Would less be passed onto him
And so I have begun to learn acceptance
And how light is born in darkness
And in this way you are my greatest teacher

Without you
I might not have had a child at all
And I might never have been forced
To face the fullness of my pain
And the lesson that vengeance
Is a lazy form of grief

Paths

If my path is not devotion
Is it gnosis or knowledge?
Maybe it is a superfluous question
For these paths are not separate
I remember
In rugby at school
Peter Perland used to say
It is better to run one yard forward
Than ten yards sideways
And so the long cut is the shortcut

Our Journey

We are wingmen
Evolving and revolving
As we spiral around Helios
Accompanying him
On his great journey
Through ups and downs
In a 225 million year orbit
Around the black hole
At the centre of our galaxy
He knows the path well
He's done it 20 times
This is our real journey
But I'm so busy
Earning a living
Or scrolling on my phone
That I forget

Being Real

Without authenticity,
How can we trust?
How can we be real
To ourselves and others?
My father used to advise me
'Trust no one, Michael.'
I didn't know how to take this
Nor where I stood
My only option was
To accept his will
And that meant
Disconnecting from myself
And the one true self
It was a survival technique
That came with hidden costs
I was rendered
Lost and blocked
And then in my relationships
When I felt hurt
I would withdraw
So that I didn't have to face the feelings
That I no longer knew how to cope with
And unable to follow my intuition
I often allowed myself to be in danger

Woke

The sound of the chickens clucking
And the dog licking himself
The feeling of the pillow under my head
The sheet over my body
The cool air on my feet that are exposed
A dryness in the mouth
As I open my eyes to
The blue light of dawn
Reach for my phone
Check the time
And open Facebook.
I catch myself and ask
Is this really what it has come to?

There is a Choice

Various parts get buried
In the dark corners of
The field of consciousness
Memories that are too agonising
Feelings that are too painful
Beliefs that stand contrary to survival
Characteristics that are not acceptable
To parents and caregivers

And so
I do not respond
To what happens
I respond to my limited perception
Of what happens

The first time
My father's unbridled rage
Was directed at me
I was about four
In a frenzy
He tried unsuccessfully
To find a key
To lock me in my bedroom
Until then
He had been
The more lenient parent

WAVES ON WAVES

But suddenly he flipped
I was terrified
And my mother became distant
Giving space for his anger
With later events
The fear and pain was greater
And I had to block out these feelings

And so
I do not see you
I see how I see you
And here the need for union
Is a problem

It has been a long road
To reconnect
To accept
And still my prejudices
Are sculpted from
The original and primitive
Acts of self-defence

Let's Suppose

Contemplating the energy
Of the trillions of stars
Their heat and light
Radiating out into the darkness
The universe is spirit
It is mind
It is intelligence
A womb
That keeps on
Birthing galaxies
And stars
And life
According to
Some mysterious algorithm
They say stars turn
Helium into hydrogen,
That fuses into carbon and oxygen
And the biggest stars m
Make neon, magnesium,
Silicon and iron
Finally they die and become supernovae
That create the rest of the material
That exists in our world
I figure it's best to take this
As a message of encouragement
To bear the weight of consciousness
To keep the house tidy

WAVES ON WAVES

And remain calm in traffic jams

Eleusis

Bless the altered states
The radical, exotic states
Visionary states
And the machine elves
Grandma, Grandad, and Uncle
And the spirits we meet
Who care for our wellbeing
Reveal how we were born
And bid us to share our gifts
To return to our natural
State of awe

In a Deeper Realm

The damage you do to me
Is damage you do to yourself
And the damage I do to you
Is damage I do to myself
There are no winners in war
And justifications are hollow
Among the screams and tears
Of suffering people
In the face of this insanity
I offer a prayer
For us to go gently
And consider
How it might feel
One day
To say we
And mean
All people
It is a challenge of universal proportions
And what stands in the way?
Divisive ideologies
Us and them thinking
Toxic human dominance hierarchies
And meanwhile we blame the other
Some other
And we hurt
We maim
We kill

We take revenge on this other
Only to find another and another

Don't miss out!

Visit the website below and you can sign up to receive emails whenever Michael Jack Simkin publishes a new book. There's no charge and no obligation.

https://books2read.com/r/B-A-VTDIB-FJFCF

BOOKS 2 READ

Connecting independent readers to independent writers.

About the Author

Born and educated in England, Michael Jack Simkin is a left-handed creative, writer, and musician. He spent years travelling around the world, experiencing shamanic journeys, spiritual practices and therapies. Today, he lives in Israel with his son and works as a marketing consultant. Simkin has written one novel and three collections of poetry.